LIFE IN ANCIENT CIVILIZATIONS

The Romans

LIFE IN ANCIENT ROME

by **Liz Sonneborn**

illustrated by **Samuel Hiti**

M Millbrook Press · Minneapolis

contents

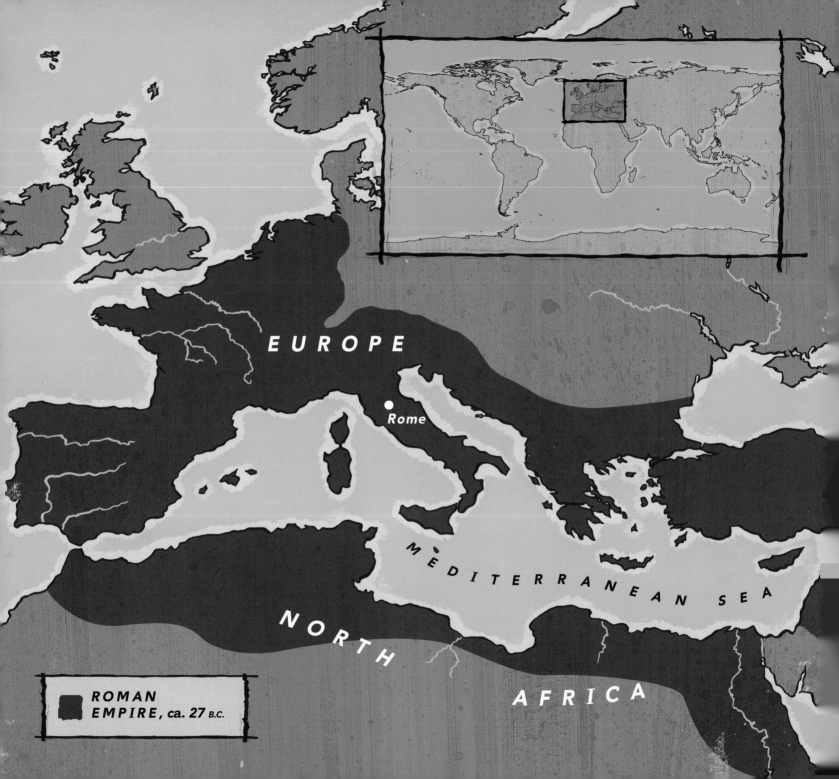

EUROPE

● Rome

MEDITERRANEAN SEA

NORTH

AFRICA

ROMAN
EMPIRE, ca. 27 B.C.

Introduction

In 753 B.C., the city of Rome was founded. The ancient Romans were clever people. They built great temples, arenas, and roads. They used the same alphabet and calendar we still use.

The Romans also had a powerful army. Over time, they gained control over many peoples and places. By 27 B.C., Rome ruled a great empire. It included lands stretching over much of Europe, Asia, and Africa.

About 1,500 years ago, the Roman Empire came to an end. But the city of Rome remains. It is now the capital of the modern country of Italy.

CHAPTER ONE

Everyday Life

Ancient Rome was a large city. Three classes, or groups, of people made up its population. A few Romans were very rich. They lived in mansions.

Wealthy Romans had many slaves to care for their homes. Some Romans had hundreds of slaves. Slaves were often captured in war. Most slaves had difficult lives. They had to do whatever their masters told them to do.

Most Romans were commoners. They lived in small houses or apartments. But these homes were not plain. Paintings often decorated the walls. Mosaics covered the floors. These designs were made from colorful stones.

This mosaic is at the entrance of a house in Pompeii, a city south of Rome. The writing warns visitors to "beware of the dog."

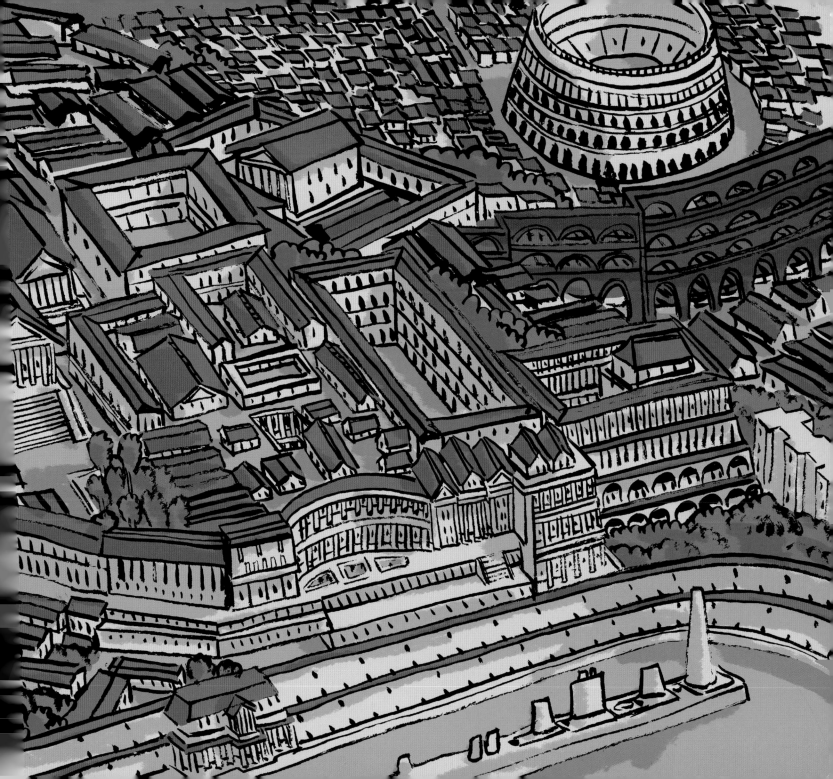

Romans loved to eat. Bread, eggs, grapes, figs, and cheese were common foods. Many Romans ate three meals a day, although the poor might skip breakfast. Dinner was the main meal.

Roman farmers grew many different food crops. The most important were wheat, olives, and grapes. Romans also raised cattle, goats, and sheep for their meat. But only rich people could afford to eat meat.

Wealthy Romans liked to attend feasts. After eating a lot of food, they sometimes made themselves throw up. With their stomachs empty, they then went back to the table for more.

At feasts, Romans laid down
on couches while they ate.

Parents educated their children at home.
Mothers taught daughters to cook and sew.
Fathers taught sons to read and write. They
also showed boys how to fight in war.

Some wealthy boys went to private school.
They studied writing, reading, and math.
Older students learned to make speeches.
(Romans expected their leaders to be
good public speakers.)

Roman students worked hard.
If they gave a wrong answer, their
teachers were allowed to hit them.

Roman children also had plenty of fun. They
played games with balls. They also loved board games.
One game was like chess.

In every household, men were in charge. Fathers had complete control over their families. They even had the right to kill a family member.

All Romans enjoyed going to public bathhouses. There, they visited with friends while lounging in steaming water. People ended a bath by plunging into a cold pool.

Men and women did not bathe together. Some bathhouses had separate sections for men and women. Others had different times of day for men and women.

Romans didn't use soap. Instead, they rubbed oil on their skin. Then they used a tool called a strigil to scrape it off.

Most Romans went to a bathhouse at least once a day. Only very wealthy people had a private bath at home.

This bathhouse is still standing in Bath, England, almost two thousand years after Romans built it.

Floors in Roman bathhouses were very hot. People wore sandals to keep their feet from burning.

The weather in Rome was often warm. To stay cool, people dressed in tunics. Tunics looked like long T-shirts, tied at the waist with a rope or belt. When Romans went outdoors, they put on sandals.

Women wore stolas over their tunics. These were long dresses. Stolas had a colorful border around the neck. Rich women sometimes wore golden earrings, rings, and necklaces.

Girls wore white clothing until they were married.
Many girls married at about the age of fourteen.

For dressy occasions, men wore white togas. A toga was one big piece of wool. Men wrapped togas around their bodies. Togas were like business suits in ancient Rome.

CHAPTER TWO

Worshipping the Gods

Romans believed in many gods and goddesses. The most powerful was Jupiter. He was the god of the sky. His wife was Juno. She was the goddess of marriage. Romans often requested help from the gods. A soldier might ask Mars for victory. A sailor might ask Neptune to keep him safe at sea. People tried not to anger the gods. They believed angry gods could make them get sick or have an accident.

The Romans told stories about the gods. These are called myths. In myths, the gods and goddesses act like people. In some, they argue. In others, they fall in love.

In Roman art, Neptune (left) often holds a fishing tool called a trident. Romans believed Neptune caused great storms and earthquakes.

Romans worshipped the gods at temples such as the Pantheon. Priests performed ceremonies at the temples. They tried to do everything right. They had to start over if they made even one mistake.

Each house also had a shrine. There, people honored gods that protected the household. Every day, they offered food and drink to the household gods.

The Romans celebrated many religious holidays. One favorite was Saturnalia. It honored Saturn, the god of farming. During this holiday, Romans feasted and played games.

Romans built the Pantheon in about A.D. 120. It was a temple for worshipping all Roman gods.

Saturnalia took place from December 17 to December 23. People celebrating would shout, "Io Saturnalia!"

Few Romans lived to be older than fifty years of age. When Romans died, their bodies were burned or buried. Some were buried in catacombs. These were underground cemeteries.

Many Romans believed the dead went to the underworld. They traveled there by crossing the river Styx. A ferryman named Charon took them across the river.

The catacombs of San Gennaro are located in southern Italy. They were first used in about A.D. 300.

When a Roman died, relatives placed a coin in that person's mouth. Romans believed the dead needed this money to pay Charon to take them to the underworld.

Roman travelers often learned about religions of other lands. One was Christianity. Some Romans began to practice this religion.

Rome's leaders tried to keep people from becoming Christians. Christians did not worship the Roman gods. The leaders worried that Roman gods would punish Rome because of this. At times, Roman leaders killed Christians.

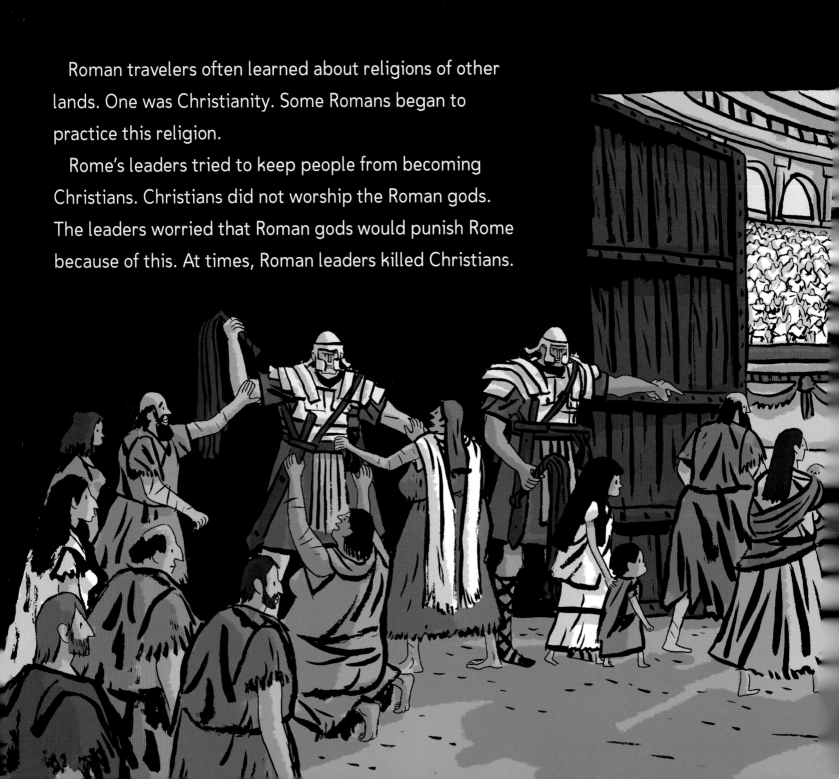

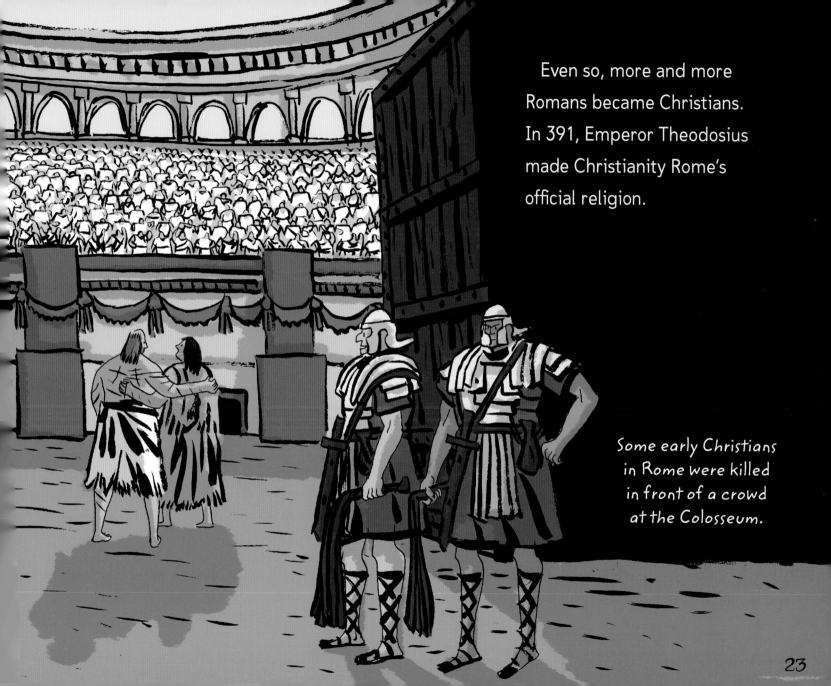

Even so, more and more Romans became Christians. In 391, Emperor Theodosius made Christianity Rome's official religion.

Some early Christians in Rome were killed in front of a crowd at the Colosseum.

23

CHAPTER THREE

Building the Roman World

The Romans were talented builders. A network of roads connected the Romans' lands. All together, there were about 370 main roads. Roman roads were very sturdy. They were paved with gravel or stone slabs. The middle was higher than the edges. That way, the roads would not flood when it rained. Instead, the water would pour into ditches dug at either side of the roads.

Romans also built bridges and tunnels. They often made them from concrete. They were the first people to use this building material. Their concrete was a mixture of sand, lime, and volcanic ash.

Romans built this road, which is located in present-day Jerash, Jordan.

The Romans built more than 53,000 miles (85,300 kilometers) of roads.

In the city of Rome, some leaders built monuments to themselves. One was the emperor Trajan, who had a column built in his honor. The column is made from marble. Pictures of Trajan's war victories are carved into it.

Rome also had many amazing buildings. There were temples, stores, and baths. Many were built around the Forum. This was a great marketplace. People came to the Forum to shop and see their friends.

Trajan's Column still stands. It is more than 100 feet (30 meters) tall.

The oldest street in Rome, the Via Sacra, ran through the Roman Forum.

One of Rome's greatest buildings was the Colosseum. It was a huge arena. The Colosseum looked a little like a football stadium. Romans gathered there to watch exciting events. They especially liked gladiator fights. Gladiators battled one another with swords. Sometimes, they fought until one of them was dead.

The gladiators who fought at the Colosseum (below) were often slaves. If a gladiator won enough fights, he might also win his freedom.

An even bigger arena was the Circus Maximus. People gathered there to watch chariot races. A chariot was a vehicle with two big wheels, pulled by a team of horses.

The best chariot drivers became rich and famous. The Roman crowds cheered for them just as sports fans do now for their favorite players.

CHAPTER FOUR

Roman Ideas and Inventions

The Roman Empire was large because of its army. Its army was the best in the world. The Roman army had more than 150,000 soldiers. The army took over foreign lands and made them part of the Roman Empire.

As the empire spread, Roman ideas also spread. Leap year, which adds an extra day to the calendar every four years, was a Roman invention. In addition, English names for the twelve months are very similar to those used by the Romans. The first three months of the year were *Januarius*, *Februarius*, and *Martius*.

Soldiers in the Roman army served for twenty to twenty-five years.

Rome was a crowded city. Several Roman inventions made the people there more comfortable. The Romans built a great sewage system. It carried dirty, smelly waste out of the city.

Plumbing was also a big concern. So the Romans built aqueducts. These structures carried water into Rome. The water ran through a channel in the aqueducts. The channel sloped downward to keep the water flowing. A huge network of pipes then carried it into each building. It took seven hundred slaves to keep the plumbing system running. They worked hard to lay down new pipes and repair old ones.

The Pont du Gard aqueduct in France is 160 feet (49 m) high. It is the tallest aqueduct the Romans built.

When they weren't fighting, Roman soldiers helped build aqueducts and other structures.

The Romans also invented a new form of government. For more than five hundred years, Rome was a republic. In a republic, the people hold the power. Romans voted for representatives to govern them. But not everyone could vote. Women, poor men, and slaves had no say in choosing Rome's leaders.

When Rome was a republic, a group called the Senate made many important decisions. Senators met in a building called the curia.

The Roman Senate usually had three hundred members. But for a time, it had more than nine hundred members.

CHAPTER FIVE

Famous Romans

Many Romans wrote books about their lives and times. From them, we know about important people in ancient Rome.

The most famous leader was Julius Caesar. Smart and brave, he was a military hero. He was also a good politician. Other politicians grew to fear him. They thought he was too powerful. Together, they stabbed him to death.

After Julius Caesar's death, his great-nephew Augustus Caesar ruled Rome. The Roman Republic was over. Augustus ruled as an all-powerful emperor. But under his rule, Rome was peaceful and prosperous.

Julius Caesar (right) lived from 100 to 44 B.C.

Romans built the Ara Pacis to celebrate how peaceful Rome was during the time when Augustus was emperor.

The Romans loved to listen to speeches. Cicero (106–43 B.C.) was famous for his. People still study his writings.

The Romans also respected poets. One of the best was Ovid (43 B.C.–A.D. 17). His greatest poem told myths about the gods and goddesses.

The best-loved Roman poet was Virgil (70–19 B.C.). He wrote a book called *The Aeneid*. It is an exciting story about a war hero named Aeneas. Even today, many people think it is one of the best books ever written.

At the end of *The Aeneid*, Aeneas fights Turnus.

CHAPTER SIX

Rome Lives On

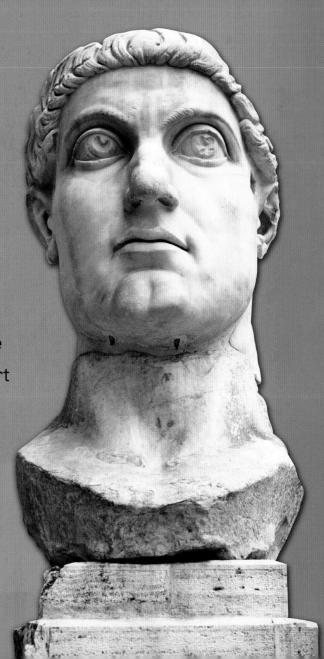

In 476, the Roman Empire came to an end. Foreigners invaded the city and took over.

Ancient Rome's civilization is gone. But we still study its history. And many museums have Roman art. There you can see beautiful Roman paintings and statues.

In the United States, some Roman ways live on. Many of our laws are based on Roman laws. The U.S. government is also similar to that of the Roman Republic. Like the Romans, we have a part of the government called the Senate.

One amazing piece of Roman art was a 30-foot-high (10 m) statue of the emperor Constantine. Its huge head is on display in Rome.

The Romans also passed on their language. It is called Latin. Very few people speak Latin now. But several modern languages are based on this language. They include Spanish, French, and Italian.

Many English words come from Latin words. They are also written using an alphabet developed by the Romans. So you can thank the Romans for the words and letters in this book.

Where ancient Rome once stood, there is now a great modern city. The new Rome is filled with tall buildings and highways. But the city also contains ruins—remains of old Roman roads and buildings. For modern Romans, these ruins are a constant reminder of the world of ancient Rome.

Modern Rome includes buildings from many different time periods. Saint Peter's Basilica (*right*) was finished in 1626.

Modern Rome has a population
of about 2,700,000.

TIMELINE

753 B.C. Romulus founds Rome.

509 B.C. The Roman Republic is formed.

202 B.C. The Romans take over lands beyond Italy.

168 B.C. The Romans take control over Greece.

73 B.C. The gladiator Spartacus unsuccessfully revolts against the Romans with other gladiators.

44 B.C. Political rivals kill Julius Caesar.

27 B.C. Augustus Caesar becomes the first Roman emperor.

A.D. 54 Nero begins his fourteen-year reign as emperor.

64 A fire destroys much of Rome.

80 Construction of the Colosseum is completed.

313 Emperor Constantine forbids the mistreatment of Christians.

391 Emperor Theodosius makes Christianity the official religion of Rome.

476 Rome falls to foreign invaders.

PRONUNCIATION GUIDE

Aeneas: ih-NEE-uhs

Aeneid: ih-NEE-uhd

aqueducts: AH-kwuh-ducks

Ara Pacis: ARE-uh PAH-kis

Caesar: SEE-zuhr

Charon: CARE-uhn

Cicero: SIH-suh-row

Colosseum: kah-luh-SEE-uhm

curia: KYUR-ee-uh

Ovid: AH-vid

Pantheon: PAN-thee-on

Saturnalia: sa-tur-NAIL-yuh

strigil: STRIH-jill

Styx: STICKS

Theodosius: thee-o-DOH-shee-uhs

toga: TOH-guh

Trajan: TRAY-jin

Virgil: VUR-jill

GLOSSARY

A.D.: *Anno Domini*. This shows that a date comes after the birth of Jesus.

ancient: very old

aqueducts: Roman structures that carried clean water into cities

B.C.: before Christ. This shows that a date comes before the birth of Jesus.

catacombs: underground cemeteries

ceremonies: religious rituals

chariot: an ancient two-wheeled vehicle pulled by a team of horses and steered by a driver

curia: a building in which the Roman Senate met

emperor: the person who governs an empire

empire: a large territory under the control of one person

gladiator: a man who fought other men in public arenas to amuse Roman crowds. Many gladiators were slaves.

lime: a chemical used in making concrete

mosaic: a design or picture made from small stones

myth: a story about ancient gods and goddesses

republic: a government ruled by representatives of the people

rivals: competitors

ruins: the remains of an old building or structure

shrine: a place where people pray to gods and goddesses

stola: a Roman woman's floor-length dress

toga: a Roman man's garment made from a single piece of wool

tunic: a T-shirt-like piece of clothing worn by Romans

underworld: the place many Romans believed the dead traveled to after they died

FURTHER READING

Biesty, Stephen. *Rome in Spectacular Cross-Section.* New York: Scholastic Reference, 2003. Describing the life of a wealthy boy named Titus, this book takes us on a trip through various Roman settings, including the Colosseum and Titus's house.

Gerrard, Roy. *The Roman Twins.* New York: Farrar, Straus and Giroux, 1998. This fun story, told in rhyme, tells the adventures of two young Roman slaves, Maximus and Vanilla.

Hodge, Susie. *Ancient Roman Art.* Des Plaines, IL: Heinemann Library, 2006. This books celebrates the work of Roman artists, from paintings to sculptures to mosaics.

James, Simon. *Ancient Rome.* New York: DK Publishing, 2004. This book features plenty of pictures of ancient Roman objects. The captions explain what the objects are and how they were used.

Macaulay, David. *City: A Story of Roman Planning and Construction.* Boston: Houghton Mifflin, 1983. Beautiful illustrations highlight Roman building techniques in the imaginary city of Verbonia.

Malam, John. *You Wouldn't Want to Be a Roman Gladiator!: Gory Things You'd Rather Not Know.* New York: Franklin Watts, 2000. This entertaining book describes the life and training of Roman gladiators.

WEBSITES

Odyssey Online: Rome
http://carlos.emory.edu/ODYSSEY/ROME/homepg.html
Art and artifacts from the Michael C. Carlos Museum of Emory University in Atlanta, Georgia, illustrate this site about Roman life.

The Roman Empire in the First Century
http://www.pbs.org/empires/romans/index.html
This website offers information on Rome as it was two thousand years ago. It features a timeline, a game, and a quiz that tells you which famous Roman you most resemble.

The Romans
http://www.bbc.co.uk/schools/romans
This site presents information and fun activities dealing with Roman life and history.

Rome Reborn
http://www.romereborn.virginia.edu
Scholars worked for ten years to create this computer simulation of ancient Rome in about A.D. 302.

INDEX

PHOTO ACKNOWLEDGMENTS

The images in this book are used with the permission of: © Bill Hauser/Independent Picture Service, p. 4; The Art Archive/Gianni Dagli Orti, p. 6; © Davis McCardle/Digital Vision/Getty Images, p. 12; © Purestock/Getty Images, p. 16; © iStockphoto.com/S. Greg Panosian, p. 18; The Art Archive/San Gennaro Catacombs Naples Italy/Gianni Dagli Orti, p. 20; © Nico Tondini/Robert Harding World Imagery/Getty Images, p. 24; © Bob Turner/Alamy, p. 26; © iStockphoto.com/Jeremy Voisey, p. 28; © Sami Sarkis/Photodisc/Getty Images, p. 32; © SuperStock, Inc./SuperStock, p. 36; © David C Tomlinson/Photographer's Choice/Getty Images, p. 40; © Ulf Sjostedt/Photographer's Choice RF/Getty Images, p. 42.

About the Illustrations

Samuel Hiti, who has a background in comic-book art, rendered the illustrations for the Life in Ancient Civilizations series using brush, ink, and computer. Hiti researched each civilization to develop distinct color palettes for these books and create his interpretations of life in these cultures.

Millbrook Press
A division of Lerner Publishing Group, Inc.
241 First Avenue North
Minneapolis, MN 55401 U.S.A.

Website address: www.lernerbooks.com

Library of Congress Cataloging-in-Publication Data

Sonneborn, Liz.
        The Romans : life in ancient Rome / by Liz Sonneborn ; illustrated by Samuel Hiti.
            p.   cm. — (Life in ancient civilizations)
        Includes index.
        ISBN: 978–0–8225–8679–1 (lib. bdg. : alk. paper)
        1. Rome—Civilization—Juvenile literature. I. Hiti, Samuel, ill. II. Title.
    DG77.S66 2010
    937—dc22   2008047788

Manufactured in the United States of America
1 2 3 4 5 6 — DP — 15 14 13 12 11 10